I0801815

BIBLE PROMISES FOR MOM

Scriptural Devotions for a Mother's Life

By Chanté Griffin

chartwell books

Quarto

© 2025 Quarto Publishing Group USA Inc.

This edition published in 2025 by Chartwell Books,
an imprint of The Quarto Group
142 West 36th Street, 4th Floor
New York, NY 10018 USA
T (212) 779-4972
www.Quarto.com

All rights reserved. No part of this book may be reproduced in any form without written permission of the copyright owners. All images in this book have been reproduced with the knowledge and prior consent of the artists concerned, and no responsibility is accepted by producer, publisher, or printer for any infringement of copyright or otherwise, arising from the contents of this publication. Every effort has been made to ensure that credits accurately comply with information supplied. We apologize for any inaccuracies that may have occurred and will resolve inaccurate or missing information in a subsequent reprinting of the book.

10 9 8 7 6 5 4 3 2 1

Chartwell titles are also available at discount for retail, wholesale, promotional, and bulk purchase. For details, contact the Special Sales Manager by email at specialsales@quarto.com or by mail at The Quarto Group, Attn: Special Sales Manager, 100 Cummings Center Suite 265D, Beverly, MA 01915, USA.

Library of Congress Control Number: 2025944459

ISBN: 978-0-7858-4795-3

Publisher: Wendy Friedman
Publishing Director: Meredith Mennitt
Editor: Joanne O'Sullivan
Designer: Alana Berry
Image credits: Shutterstock

Printed in China

CONTENTS

INTRODUCTION

Psalms 127:3 says "Children are a heritage from the LORD, offspring a reward from him." This psalm reminds us that motherhood is a gift from God. Being able to raise children is a beautiful blessing. Motherhood is challenging, whether your children are infants, teens, young adults—or if you work inside or outside of the home.

Motherhood is tricky, in part because you're balancing so much. How do you keep your children safe and healthy? How do you ensure they're well educated and well adjusted? How do you make sure they develop strong character and godly habits? And how do you do all the aforementioned and still take care of yourself in the process?

Bible Promises for Mom was designed to help you care for yourself as you care for your children. This book provides devotional topics especially relevant to mothers. The book explores each topic through key Bible verses, a brief reflection, and a prayer you can say aloud.

Some topics (Patience, Generosity, and Parenting) address motherhood directly. Other topics such as Prayer, Righteousness, Scripture, and Faith focus more on your spiritual growth. Finally, topics including Friendship, Envy, and Marriage help you tend your other relationships. Cumulatively, these topics were chosen to help you thrive as a mother and as a woman.

As a mother, you know how hard it can be to carve out enough time to care for yourself. Each devotional was designed to give you encouragement, inspiration, and teaching every day, even if you have only a few minutes. This book was designed to help you tend to your children's spiritual growth as well as your own.

In Deuteronomy 11:18–20, God spoke to the Israelites. The words he spoke to them are relevant to us today. "Fix these words of mine in your hearts and minds; tie them as symbols on your hands and bind them on your foreheads. Teach them to your children, talking about them when you sit at home, and when you walk along the road, when you lie down, and when you get up. Write them on the doorframes of your houses and on your gates,"

Bible Promises for Mom will help you keep God's words in your hearts and your minds and in the hearts and minds of your children. Let the verses within these pages inspire both you and your children when you wake up and when you go to sleep, when you're sitting around the house, and when you're out in your neighborhood. Teach these verses to your children so that when they become adults, they can do the same for their children.

Reflections, Prayers, and Scripture

JOY

Life's one certainty is this: There will always be mountain highs and valley lows, good times and bad times; times when all is well with your family, and seasons that are marked by schisms and misunderstandings, or sickness and grief. Yet joy is always available to you, as perennially present as the daily sunrise, ready to shine hope and light into the darkest of valleys. Joy is the promised gift for all who choose to sit with God in the lowest moments. Joy is the evidence of a life spent with God. So, when you experience a crushing low, take the opportunity to sit with God and receive joy.

Dear God of Comfort,

I'm grateful that you promised to bring joy into my life and my household. I pray that I will experience your joy daily, whether I'm experiencing a mountain high or a valley low. Help me to sit with you in prayer until I tangibly feel your joy.

Amen

You make known to me the path of life; you will fill me with joy in your presence, with eternal pleasures at your right hand.

PSALMS 16:11

When anxiety was great within me, your consolation brought me joy.

PSALMS 94:19

A joyful heart is good medicine, but a crushed spirit dries up the bones.

PROVERBS 17:22

Those who sow in tears shall reap with shouts of joy! He who goes out weeping, bearing the seed for sowing, shall come home with shouts of joy, bringing his sheaves with him.

PSALMS 126:5–6

Splendor and majesty are before him; strength and joy are in his dwelling place.

1 CHRONICLES 16:27

LOVE

You are loved. You are loved by God and so many others. While your role as a mother naturally compels you to show sacrificial love to your children in big and small ways, never forget that you are loved. You were loved before you were a mom, before you were born. As you reflect on the verses in this chapter, know that the love you show your children daily is but a fraction of the love God has for his children. May you know God's love in its abundance, as a child and as a mother.

Dear Heavenly Father,

I'm grateful I can love others because you first loved me. I need you to fill me with your Spirit so I can exhibit deeper levels of love. Please cultivate within me love's byproducts: patience, gentleness, and humility. Each day, help me to bear with my children and myself in love.

Amen

Hatred stirs up conflict, but love covers over all wrongs.

PROVERBS 10:12

Be completely humble and gentle; be patient, bearing with one another in love.

EPHESIANS 4:2

Love must be sincere. Hate what is evil; cling to what is good.

ROMANS 12:9

But the fruit of the Spirit is love, joy, peace, forbearance, kindness, goodness, faithfulness, gentleness and self-control. Against such things there is no law.

GALATIANS 5:22–23

And now these three remain: faith, hope and love. But the greatest of these is love.

1 CORINTHIANS 13:13

RIGHTEOUSNESS

Righteousness, being in right standing with God, is a gift to all who entrust their lives to Christ Jesus. From the Old Testament to the New Testament, Scripture promises that those who seek after righteousness will find it, and that those who find it are blessed. But in a world that mocks righteousness and instead reveres money, power, and fame, righteousness doesn't always look attractive. Yet Scripture invites us to treasure righteousness and to put it on like beautiful, fine clothing.

Righteous Father,

Clothe me in your righteousness. Give me the desire and the humility to ask for it, even when it feels countercultural. Show me how to live a righteous life and teach me how to show my children as well. I want my entire family to live blessed, righteous lives.

Amen

Whoever walks in integrity walks securely, but whoever takes crooked paths will be found out.

PROVERBS 10:9

Whoever pursues righteousness and kindness will find life, righteousness, and honor.

PROVERBS 21:21

The eyes of the Lord are on the righteous, and his ears are attentive to their cry.

PSALMS 34:15

Blessed are those who hunger and thirst for righteousness, for they will be filled.

MATTHEW 5:6

Blessed are those who are persecuted because of righteousness, for theirs is the kingdom of heaven.

MATTHEW 5:10

SCRIPTURE

How do you view your Scripture reading time? Do you see it as an item to check off your daily to-do list, or as the most important meal of the day? Do you nibble on it all day long, like you would your favorite snack? The Bible tells us that God's Word is our daily bread. Scripture is meant to encourage us, correct us, and teach us. It shows us which path to take, as well as which to avoid. Scripture fills us up with hope in a world filled up with darkness. When we gladly feast on the Word daily, we realize we don't need to look anywhere else for sustenance because we have all that we need.

Father God,

Help me to see your words as the most important meal of my day. Increase my desire to read and meditate on your Word throughout my day: when I wake up, as I drive, while I cook dinner, and when I prepare for bed. Help me to set an example that my children will follow.

Amen

For everything that was written in the past was written to teach us, so that through the endurance taught in the Scriptures and the encouragement they provide we might have hope.

ROMANS 15:4

Jesus answered, "It is written: 'Man shall not live on bread alone, but on every word that comes from the mouth of God.'"

MATTHEW 4:4

Let the message of Christ dwell among you richly as you teach and admonish one another with all wisdom through psalms, hymns, and songs from the Spirit, singing to God with gratitude in your hearts.

COLOSSIANS 3:16

Your word is a lamp for my feet, a light on my path.

PSALMS 119:105

All Scripture is God-breathed and is useful for teaching, rebuking, correcting and training in righteousness.

2 TIMOTHY 3:16

MERCY

Mercy is a reflection and extension of God's love. Mercy is God's limitless kindness and compassion to those who need it and those who don't deserve it. The Bible teaches that God is rich in mercy and displays it "upon generation after generation" (Luke 1:50). Yet God requires us to give the same mercy we've received, lest it be taken away. So today practice being merciful to your children, your friends, your neighbors, and yourself. Give everyone you encounter the precious gift of mercy.

Dear Loving God,

Your love for me is so great that you show mercy to me daily. I pray that each day I would see just how merciful you are to me and that I would extend that same mercy to those I interact with. Teach me how to show more mercy to my children when they mess up.

Amen

For I will forgive their wickedness and will remember their sins no more.

HEBREWS 8:12

Blessed are the merciful, for they will be shown mercy.

MATTHEW 5:7

Because judgment without mercy will be shown to anyone who has not been merciful. Mercy triumphs over judgment.

JAMES 2:13

The Lord is gracious and compassionate, slow to anger and rich in love.

PSALMS 145:8

Mercy, peace, and love be yours in abundance.

JUDE 1:2

HOPE

When the storms of life wreak havoc on you, sometimes it's hard to hope that things will ultimately be okay. Yet this is when hope is most needed. Hope is light in a dark, stormy night; and hope is the air we need to breathe when life has knocked the wind out of us. Hope reminds us that after the storm, the sun always shines again. When our hope is in God, we can confidently hold his hand during any storm, knowing that our lives, both physical and eternal, are always secure.

God of all Hope,

I'm thankful that your Spirit gives me the ability to hope, even when circumstances seem hopeless. I need you to show me how to cultivate hope. When the storms rage, help me to pray and meditate on your Word until I feel hope rise within me.

Amen

Why, my soul, are you downcast? Why so disturbed within me?
Put your hope in God, for I will yet praise him, my Savior and my God.

PSALMS 42:11

May the God of hope fill you with all joy and peace as you trust in him, so that you may overflow with hope by the power of the Holy Spirit.

ROMANS 15:13

Let us hold unswervingly to the hope we profess, for he who promised is faithful.

HEBREWS 10:23

We have this hope as an anchor for the soul, firm and secure. It enters the inner sanctuary behind the curtain.

HEBREWS 6:19

We are hard pressed on every side but not crushed; perplexed, but not in despair; persecuted but not abandoned; struck down but not destroyed. We always carry around in our body the death of Jesus, so that the life of Jesus may also be revealed in our body.

2 CORINTHIANS 4:8–10

SIN

Sin is a little word with big consequences. The topic of sin makes some people feel uncomfortable because they're 'good people.' Yet Scripture teaches that all have sinned, and more importantly—that Jesus died and rose to save us from our sins. Through this salvation we receive the power to resist sin and the gift to confess when we've not resisted. Scripture promises that as we do this, our sins will be forgiven, and we will be blessed.

Forgiving Father,

I'm grateful that you continuously forgive all my sins, whether I commit them intentionally or unintentionally. I pray that you would cleanse the things inside me that consistently choose sin instead of you. If and when I fall, please help me to be quick to confess and receive your grace and forgiveness.

Amen

Just as people are destined to die once, and after that to face judgment, so Christ was sacrificed once to take away the sins of many; and he will appear a second time, not to bear sin, but to bring salvation to those who are waiting for him.

HEBREWS 9:27–28

Therefore, rid yourselves of all malice, deceit, hypocrisy, envy, and slander of every kind.

1 PETER 2:1

If we confess our sins, he is faithful and just and will forgive us our sins and purify us from all unrighteousness.

1 JOHN 1:9

Blessed is the one whose transgressions are forgiven, whose sins are covered.

PSALM 32:1

If we claim to be without sin, we deceive ourselves and the truth is not in us.

1 JOHN 1:8

FRIENDSHIP

Friendship is forged over time; over long conversations, coffee dates, house visits, and extended phone calls. In the book of John, Jesus calls his disciples his friends, and we see him model a deep friendship by serving them, praying for them, too, and sharing vulnerably about his life. We, too, can experience this type of friendship with other women, older and younger. We can cook food for them, pray over them, and share the intimate details of our lives; and we will find that they do the same for us. Over time, we will see that two or three or four is better than one.

God,

I'm thankful that you call me your friend and that you don't withhold parts of yourself from me. I pray that I will be to others what you have been to me. I pray that I will serve sacrificially, share courageously, and pray consistently. Always out of love, never out of obligation.

Amen

He who withholds kindness from a friend forsakes the fear of the almighty.

JOB 6:14

Perfume and incense bring joy to the heart, and the pleasantness of a friend springs from their heartfelt advice.

PROVERBS 27:9

My command is this: love one another as I have loved you.

JOHN 15:12-13

Walk with the wise and become wise, for a companion of fools suffers harm.

PROVERBS 13:20

WORLDLINESS

We live in a society that is consumed with making more and having more. Worldliness is pursuing more for you and your family while giving less to the family of God. Worldliness keeps you preoccupied with building your own "queendom" instead of building God's kingdom. To say 'no' to worldliness and 'yes' to godliness, you must allow God to transform your mind so that your thoughts align with his. You must allow him to transform your smaller worldview into an expansive kingdom view.

God,

You know how easy it is for me to stay focused on my own plans and desires that I neglect yours. Please transform my mind so that it is characterized by godliness, not worldliness. Please show me how to live this out daily alongside my family and children.

Amen

For the love of money is a root of all kinds of evil. Some people, eager for money, have wandered from the faith and pierced themselves with many griefs.

1 TIMOTHY 6:10

But the Lord said to Samuel, "Do not look on his appearance or on the height of his stature, because I have rejected him. For the Lord sees not as man sees: man looks on the outward appearance, but the Lord looks on the heart."

1 SAMUEL 16:7

Do not conform to the pattern of this world but be transformed by the renewing of your mind. Then you will be able to test and approve what God's will is—his good, pleasing and perfect will.

ROMANS 12:2

For the grace of God has appeared that offers salvation to all people. It teaches us to say "no" to ungodliness and worldly passions, and to live self-controlled, upright and godly lives in this present age.

TITUS 2:11-12

GENEROSITY

Generosity is a sign that love is flowing: between us and God and us and others. Generosity is the cornerstone of our faith and the cornerstone of healthy relationships. When you consistently experience God's generosity to you, you can't help but respond by giving just as generously to those around you. Giving liberally is a sign that God's love dwells in you. It's also a sign that God is pleased with you.

Father,

I thank you that generosity is a part of your nature. I'm in awe of how you love your children and give so generously to us, without any expectation of reciprocation. Help me to live a life of generosity, whether I'm interacting with my children and family, or encountering a stranger on the street. Help me to be generous with my time, energy, and money.

Amen

May the Lord make your love increase and overflow for each other and for everyone else, just as ours does for you.

1 THESSALONIANS 3:12

Each of you should give what you have decided in your heart to give, not reluctantly or under compulsion, for God loves a cheerful giver.

2 CORINTHIANS 9:7

And do not forget to do good and to share with others, for with such sacrifices God is pleased.

HEBREWS 13:16

Give, and it will be given to you. A good measure, pressed down, shaken together, running over, will be put into your lap. For with the measure you use, it will be measured to you.

LUKE 6:38

They [the righteous] are always generous and lend freely; their children will be a blessing.

PSALMS 37:26

PATIENCE

Patience truly is a virtue. Patience reveals love and humility, because when you display patience, you don't lord a person's shortcomings over them. Instead, you bear with them in love. A patient mom prays, not just for her child to grow in character and maturity, but for her heart to exhibit love, even if some character traits never change. Being patient with your child is especially challenging because your job is to model patience while disciplining them so they can learn godly character. Perhaps the best way to model patience to them, then, is to be patient with yourself when your parenting, like your child, proves it's not perfect.

Dear Father,

Many times, I struggle to show love through patience, both to my child and to myself. Help me to hold our shortcomings with love. Show me how patient you are with me and teach me how to be the same with my family.

Amen

Love is patient, love is kind. It does not envy, it does not boast, it is not proud. It does not dishonor others, it is not self-seeking, it is not easily angered, it keeps no record of wrongs. Love does not delight in evil but rejoices with the truth. It always protects, always trusts, always hopes, always perseveres.
Love never fails. But where there are prophecies, they will cease; where there are tongues, they will be stilled; where there is knowledge, it will pass away.

1 CORINTHIANS 13:4–8

Be patient, then, brothers and sisters, until the Lord's coming. See how the farmer waits for the land to yield its valuable crop, patiently waiting for the autumn and spring rains.

JAMES 5:7

The Lord will fight for you; you need only to be still.

EXODUS 14:14

And the Lord's servant must not be quarrelsome but must be kind to everyone, able to teach, not resentful. Opponents must be gently instructed, in the hope that God will grant them repentance leading them to a knowledge of the truth.

2 TIMOTHY 2:24–25

CONFLICT

Where there's great conflict in relationships, there's little peace. Peace in relationships soothes your soul, but conflict agitates it. Conflict divides and builds friction, yet it is inevitable in most relationships. So learning to manage conflict is a life-long journey. Intentionally working to control your anger, choosing to be kind when you've been hurt, and deciding to forgive—no matter what—are head decisions as much as they are heart decisions. Allow Jesus, who promises to be your peace, to teach you.

God,

I'll admit sometimes I allow conflict to stew because I don't want to confront a situation, while other times I fuel conflict because I'm angry and don't want to forgive. I need you to give me the courage to confront and the courage to forgive. I want a life marked by peace, not conflict.

Amen

Get rid of all bitterness, rage and anger, brawling and slander, along with every form of malice. Be kind and compassionate to one another, forgiving each other, just as in Christ God forgave you.

EPHESIANS 4:31-32

Rescue me, Lord, from evildoers; protect me from the violent, who devise evil plans in their hearts and stir up war every day.

PSALMS 140:1-2

Better a patient person than a warrior, one with self-control than one who takes a city.

PROVERBS 16:32

For he himself is our peace, who has made the two groups one and has destroyed the barrier, the dividing wall of hostility.

EPHESIANS 2:14

Make every effort to live in peace with everyone and to be holy; without holiness no one will see the Lord.

HEBREWS 12:14

ENVY

Envy packs a huge punch because it negatively affects our relationships with God and with other people. When envious, we covet what others have instead of celebrating their accomplishments and milestones. When envious, we (silently) complain about what we haven't received instead of being grateful for what God has given us. The most insidious effect of envy might be that it keeps our eyes focused on material things instead of eternal things. In essence, envy fixes our eyes on the kingdoms of this world instead of on God's kingdom. Envy keeps us brooding over what we don't have instead of humbly asking God for what we want.

Giving God,

Your forgiveness, like your generosity, knows no bounds. Please forgive me for the times I've been jealous and envious of others: those I know personally and those on social media. Please root out the source of my envy and plant seeds of gratitude inside of me. Help me to be content with what you've already blessed my family with until you decide to give us more.

Amen

You are still worldly. For since there is jealousy and quarreling among you, are you not worldly? Are you not acting like mere humans?

1 CORINTHIANS 3:3

A heart at peace gives life to the body, but envy rots the bones.

PROVERBS 14:30

And I saw that all toil and all achievement spring from one person's envy of another. This too is meaningless, a chasing after the wind.

ECCLESIASTES 4:4

Then he said to them, "Watch out! Be on your guard against all kinds of greed; life does not consist in an abundance of possessions."

LUKE 12:15

Anger is cruel and fury overwhelming, but who can stand before jealousy?

PROVERBS 27:4

DOUBT

Christianity is founded on the belief and faith that Jesus is the Son of God and that nothing is impossible with God. Doubt, however, says that there are some things God can't do. Doubt often arises when you face a difficult situation or circumstance that seems impossible to overcome. When doubt creeps in like a thief in the night, your faith in God's power will offer protection. Clinging to faith will ensure it isn't snatched from your hands. Praying and reading Scripture about God's power will help you to hold onto faith. Clinging to faith instead of doubt ensures that doubt never becomes your god.

Father God,

Too often I doubt and forget that you are all-powerful. Too often I allow doubt to taint my mind and my emotions. Please help me to combat doubt with faith. Daily, show me just how powerful you are.

Amen

But when you ask, you must believe and not doubt, because the one who doubts is like a wave of the sea, blown and tossed by the wind.

JAMES 1:6

Trust in the Lord with all your heart, and do not lean on your own understanding. In all your ways acknowledge him, and he will make straight your paths.

PROVERBS 3:5–6

And without faith it is impossible to please God, because anyone who comes to him must believe that he exists and that he rewards those who earnestly seek him.

HEBREWS 11:6

Truly I tell you, if anyone says to this mountain, "Go, throw yourself into the sea," and does not doubt in their heart but believes that what they say will happen, it will be done for them.

MARK 11:23

SERVANTHOOD

As a mom, it's tempting to put everyone else's needs above yours—all in the name of servanthood. This can lead to burnout and eventually bitterness. Servanthood, like most good things, requires boundaries. We see this modeled by Jesus, the servant of all. Throughout Scripture, we see Jesus' servanthood interspersed with physical and spiritual rest. In Mark 4:36, Jesus serves the crowds and then goes away, presumably to rest. In Mark 6:46, Jesus serves and then goes away to pray and commune with his father. We are to do the same. Serve our families and rest. Care for our children and steal away to pray, even if just for a few minutes.

Giving God,

I thank you that Jesus is the model for servanthood and for rest. Help me not just to serve my family, but to also prioritize rest and time with you. Help me to place boundaries around my servanthood so that I can enjoy being the servant of all.

Amen

But be sure to fear the Lord and serve him faithfully with all your heart; consider what great things he has done for you.

1 SAMUEL 12:24

Sitting down, Jesus called the Twelve and said, "Anyone who wants to be first must be the very last, and the servant of all."

MARK 9:35

Religion that God our Father accepts as pure and faultless is this: to look after orphans and widows in their distress and to keep oneself from being polluted by the world.

JAMES 1:27

And we know that for those who love God all things work together for good, for those who are called according to his purpose.

ROMANS 8:28

PARENTING

Parenting is the toughest job you'll ever have, hands down. You do so much for your children: feed them, teach them, correct them, protect them. Yet sometimes they aren't grateful for any of it. Sometimes, they're downright hostile towards you because of it. During these times it's imperative to remember that children are a heritage from God, and that it's a privilege and a reward, no matter how hard it gets, to parent your children physically, emotionally, and spiritually, to continue to teach and train them, especially when they don't like it. Their resistance to your teaching is often proof they really need it. So, persevere in parenting, in teaching, and in praying for your children. Their future selves need you.

Father God,

I thank you that my children are a heritage and a reward. I thank you for the opportunity to parent them, even when it's challenging. Help me to push through the hard times and give me the wisdom to parent well. I pray that my children grow up to be God-honoring adults who raise God-honoring children.

Amen

Teach them to your children, talking about them when you sit at home and when you walk along the road, when you lie down and when you get up.

DEUTERONOMY 11:19

Only be careful and watch yourselves closely so that you do not forget the things your eyes have seen or let them fade from your heart as long as you live. Teach them to your children and to their children after them.

DEUTERONOMY 4:9

Start children off on the way they should go, and even when they are old they will not turn from it.

PROVERBS 22:6

Children are a heritage from the Lord, offspring a reward from him.

PSALMS 127:3

OPEN-HEARTEDNESS

An open heart is the gateway to deep, intimate relationships. Having an open heart enables you to receive an abundance of love from God, friends and family, and sometimes even strangers on the street! Sometimes, it feels easier to close your heart, though. Disappointment, hurt, and betrayal can make you want to place a permanent 'do not enter' sign over your heart. But banning entry into your heart keeps you from receiving and giving love. If you're struggling to open up, remember that you can entrust your heart to God fully, knowing that he specializes in healing wounded, broken hearts. Allow God to show you how to deal with past hurts and keep your heart open so you can continue to give and receive love in all your relationships.

Loving God,

It's amazing how big and open your heart is, despite how much you've been hurt and betrayed. I need you to heal the parts of my heart that have been injured and fear being hurt again. I also need you to help me to forgive. Teach me how to be openhearted to everyone: from family and friends who've hurt me to strangers on the street.

Amen

But love your enemies, do good to them, and lend to them without expecting to get anything back. Then your reward will be great, and you will be children of the Most High, because he is kind to the ungrateful and wicked.

LUKE 6:35

Defend the weak and the fatherless; uphold the cause of the poor and the oppressed.

PSALMS 82:3

But whenever anyone turns to the Lord, the veil is taken away.

2 CORINTHIANS 3:16

He heals the brokenhearted and binds up their wounds.

PSALMS 147:3

Trust in the Lord with all your heart and lean not on your own understanding; in all your ways submit to him, and he will make your paths straight.

PROVERBS 3:5-6

MOTHERHOOD

Mothering is like the farmer who sows seed into the four soils (Mark 4). As a mother, you sow discipline and self-control into your child and hope that they grow. You sow compassion, respect, and good manners, and hope that they grow for years to come. You sow a love for God and love for neighbors and hope that they take root. As a mother, you also pray incessantly: that all the seed you've sown is neither eaten by birds nor scorched by the sun. You pray that the seed you've sown falls on soil that has depth and no thorns. You pray that all the seed you've sown into your child falls on good soil so it can grow and produce a bountiful, beautiful crop!

God,

I pray that you would teach me how best to sow seed into my child. I pray also that you would teach me how to cultivate the soil of my child's heart. Would you nurture and protect the soil from everything destructive? I pray that my child's heart would be good soil for all the good seed sown.

Amen

I have no greater joy than to hear that my children are walking in the truth.

3 JOHN 1:4

Her children arise and call her blessed; her husband also, and he praises her: Many women do noble things, but you surpass them all. Charm is deceptive, and beauty is fleeting; but a woman who fears the Lord is to be praised. Honor her for all that her hands have done and let her works bring her praise at the city gate.

PROVERBS 31:28–31

As a mother comforts her child, so will I comfort you; and you will be comforted over Jerusalem.

ISAIAH 66:13

Be sure you know the condition of your flocks, give careful attention to your herds.

PROVERBS 27:23

PRAYER

It can be hard to believe that the God who created the universe wants to spend time with you every day in prayer. It's easy to wonder: Does God want to hear from me, and, if so, will He answer my prayers? The only way to know is to try it—to spend time praying to God. Daily, thank God for the blessings in your life and what you're grateful for. Then confess the things you're afraid of and worried about; and ask God to intervene. You'll find that God is in fact powerful and that your prayers are in fact potent. Praying will reveal that the God who created the universe is neither far away nor distant, but rather close and personal.

God of the Universe,

I want to pray more but sometimes struggle to prioritize it. Please increase both my discipline and my desire to pray. Teach me how to share my deepest sorrows and joys with you. Show me how powerfully you can show up in my life when I show up in prayer.

Amen

Rejoice always, pray continually, give thanks in all circumstances; for this is God's will for you in Christ Jesus.

1 THESSALONIANS 5:16-18

Then you will call upon me and come and pray to me, and I will hear you.

JEREMIAH 29:12

If you believe, you will receive whatever you ask for in prayer.

MATTHEW 21:22

Therefore, confess your sins to each other and pray for each other so that you may be healed. The prayer of a righteous person is powerful and effective.

JAMES 5:16

WORRY

Worry accomplishes nothing, and it is the antithesis of peace. Yet you may worry a lot: about your kids, family, finances, and future. Will my family be okay? What about next year? Ten years from now? The good thing is that worry stems from concern, so you can choose to channel that concern differently. You can choose to cast your concerns and anxieties onto God. Tell God what you're concerned about and why. Ask God to override any worry with peace. Ask God to work the troubling situation out for good. As you practice casting your concerns onto God, you'll notice that your days feel lighter and peace-filled.

Father God,

Thank you for being the God of peace. You promise to bring peace to me if I bring my worries to you, so help me to cast my concerns onto you. Each day help me to choose prayer over panic and peace over anxiety.

Amen

Therefore, do not worry about tomorrow, for tomorrow will worry about itself. Each day has enough trouble of its own.

MATTHEW 6:34

Casting all your anxieties on him; because he cares for you.

1 PETER 5:7

Can any one of you add a single hour to your life by worrying?

MATTHEW 6:27

Do not be anxious about anything, but in every situation, by prayer and petition, with thanksgiving, present your requests to God. And the peace of God, which transcends all understanding, will guard your hearts and your minds in Christ Jesus.

PHILIPPIANS 4:6-7

COMPASSION

Compassion is contagious. If we cultivate it inside our homes, it can spread outside our homes. Inside our homes we must choose: will we tenderly correct our children after they've disobeyed us for the tenth time that day? Or will we yell at them in anger? Will we choose to demonstrate compassion to them when they don't listen, just like God shows compassion to us when we're disobedient? Let's practice showing compassion to our children first, inside of our homes, so they can extend it to others at school, church, and beyond.

Compassionate God,

You are the ultimate model of compassion. Please help me to be compassionate with my children, especially when they mess up and anger me. In these moments help me to model forgiveness and gentleness. Help me to be more like you.

Amen

Defend the weak and the fatherless; uphold the cause of the poor and the oppressed.

PSALMS 82:3

He is able to deal gently with those who are ignorant and are going astray, since he himself is subject to weakness.

HEBREWS 5:2

Do not gloat when your enemy falls; when they stumble, do not let your heart rejoice.

PROVERBS 24:17

Therefore, as God's chosen people, holy and dearly loved, clothe yourselves with compassion, kindness, humility, gentleness and patience.

COLOSSIANS 3:12

PERSEVERANCE

Perseverance is the path to the life you want and the life God wants for you. Perseverance doesn't come easily, though. In fact, the things you want the most—a strong, healthy body; thriving children, and a close relationship with God—all necessitate perseverance. Perseverance requires discipline, determination, and an unwillingness to quit. Think about it: eating healthy food and exercising regularly require discipline. Studying Scripture and praying regularly require determination. Consistently teaching and disciplining your children requires an unwillingness to quit. It's all worth it because the more you persevere, the more you see the fruit of perseverance in your life, and the more you experience God's best for you.

Father God,

I want the life you have for me, but I confess: I need more discipline and determination. Teach me the value of perseverance and help me to practice it in every area, including my health and fitness, my spiritual disciplines, and my parenting. I want to persevere more for myself and my children.

Amen

But as for you, be strong and do not give up, for your work will be rewarded.

2 CHRONICLES 15:7

So do not throw away your confidence; it will be richly rewarded. You need to persevere so that when you have done the will of God, you will receive what he has promised.

HEBREWS 10:35-36

Consider it pure joy, my brothers and sisters, whenever you face trials of many kinds, because you know that the testing of your faith produces perseverance. Let perseverance finish its work so that you may be mature and complete, not lacking anything.

JAMES 1:2-4

Fixing our eyes on Jesus, the pioneer and perfecter of faith. For the joy set before him he endured the cross, scorning its shame, and sat down at the right hand of the throne of God.

HEBREWS 12:2

She watches over the affairs of her household and does not eat the bread of idleness.

PROVERBS 31:27

COVENANT

A covenant is essentially a contract between parties. Most of the covenants in the Bible are between God and his children. Some covenants are conditional, meaning God promises to do something if his children obey. Other covenants are unconditional, meaning God promises to do something, no matter what. As a mother you understand the power of 'if-then' contracts with your child. "If you clean your room, then I will drive you to your friend's birthday party." As a mother, there's also an innate, unconditional covenant you've made with your child. "I will always love you, always do what's best for you. You are mine." Biblical covenants remind us how much we're loved by God and how much God wants to show us with good things, if only we'd obey!

Loving God,

I'm grateful that like you, I love my children without condition. As a mom I also understand the importance of setting conditional covenants with children. But I admit: I don't always want to adhere to the terms of your covenants. Sometimes I don't want to listen to you. For that I ask for forgiveness. Help me to obey your covenants and receive the good things you have for me and my family.

Amen

"Though the mountains be shaken and the hills be removed, yet my unfailing love for you will not be shaken nor my covenant of peace be removed," says the Lord, who has compassion on you.

ISAIAH 54:10

Now if you obey me fully and keep my covenant, then out of all nations you will be my treasured possession. Although the whole earth is mine.

EXODUS 19:5

Know therefore that the Lord your God is God; he is the faithful God, keeping his covenant of love to a thousand generations of those who love him and keep his commandments.

DEUTERONOMY 7:9

"This is the covenant I will make with them after that time," says the Lord. "I will put my laws in their hearts, and I will write them on their minds."

HEBREWS 10:16

I have set my rainbow in the clouds, and it will be the sign of the covenant between me and the earth.

GENESIS 9:13

It was not with our ancestors that the Lord made this covenant, but with us, with all of us who are alive here today.

DEUTERONOMY 5:3

SUFFERING

No one likes to suffer. No wonder: suffering is often accompanied by darkness, depression, and feelings of isolation. However, Scripture reveals that suffering is an essential element of the Christian life. Jesus suffered so we can have a new, resurrected life; so we, too, must suffer to receive that resurrected life. All suffering isn't created equal, though. Jesus invites us into the suffering that leads to a new life—in us and others. With this type of suffering, God's glory can shine through because the thing designed to bring death ultimately produces life. Suffering, in God's hands, is meant to be life-giving.

All-Powerful God,

I don't like to suffer and I maybe never will, but I don't want to be afraid of suffering because it's inevitable. Instead, please help me to turn to you in times of intense suffering. Please help me to push through the pain to receive the new, resurrected life you have for me.

Amen

But rejoice, insofar as you share Christ's sufferings, that you may also rejoice and be glad when his glory is revealed.

1 PETER 4:13

I consider that the sufferings of this present time are not worth comparing with the glory that is to be revealed to us.

ROMANS 8:18

Do not be afraid of what you are about to suffer. I tell you, the devil will put some of you in prison to test you, and you will suffer persecution for ten days. Be faithful, even to the point of death, and I will give you life as your victor's crown.

REVELATION 2:10

But even if you should suffer for what is right, you are blessed. Do not fear their threats; do not be frightened.

1 PETER 3:14

In fact, everyone who wants to live a godly life in Christ Jesus will be persecuted.

2 TIMOTHY 3:12

And whoever does not carry their cross and follow me cannot be my disciple.

LUKE 14:27

SALVATION

Salvation is a gift for all who choose to trust in Jesus, our Good Shepherd. Thankfully a good shepherd's care and salvation of his flock is ongoing. A good shepherd feeds his sheep, saving them from hunger and famine. A good shepherd leads the sheep to green pastures and flowing water. When the sheep are exhausted, the good shepherd makes them rest. This shepherd also stands guard and saves the sheep from outside predators that would try to break into the sheep-pen. Finally, if the sheep try to leave the sheep-pen, the shepherd disciplines them—not to punish, but to protect. Their complete salvation and care are the shepherd's top priority. Are you allowing the Good Shepherd to bring salvation into every area of your life?

Lord,

I'm the sheep that's constantly in need of a good shepherd. Often, I try to take care of myself and my family, alone. Would you help me to welcome your care and salvation into every part of my life?

Amen

Surely God is my salvation; I will trust and not be afraid. The Lord, the Lord himself, is my strength and my defense; he has become my salvation.

ISAIAH 12:2

In the same way, I tell you, there is rejoicing in the presence of the angels of God over one sinner who repents.

LUKE 15:10

And everyone who calls on the name of the Lord will be saved.

ACTS 2:21

For the grace of God has appeared that offers salvation to all people. It teaches us to say 'no' to ungodliness and worldly passions, and to live self-controlled, upright and godly lives in this present age, while we wait for the blessed hope—the appearing of the glory of our great God and Savior, Jesus Christ, who gave himself for us to redeem us from all wickedness and to purify for himself a people that are his very own, eager to do what is good.

TITUS 2:11-14

HOLINESS

Simply put, holiness is being set apart for God and God's plans. Because holiness is multi-dimensional, it affects how we relate to God, others, and ourselves. Being holy means we consistently choose the thing that honors God, despite how we feel. Holiness asks us to present our bodies as living sacrifices (Romans 12:1), which means we refuse to indulge in sins like gluttony and sexual immorality. Holiness also means that we do our best to maintain peaceful and loving relationships with everyone, despite how they've treated us (Romans 12:18). Holiness feels attainable when we recognize that God alone has the power to give us both the desire and the ability to live a set apart life.

Holy God,

Sometimes holiness feels like a heavy, unattainable weight; but your invitation into holiness is really protection from sin's dire consequences. Would you give me the desire and ability to live a set apart life that strengthens my relationships with you, others, and myself?

Amen

Don't you know that you yourselves are God's temple and that God's Spirit dwells in your midst?

1 CORINTHIANS 3:16

That we, being delivered from the hand of our enemies, might serve him without fear, in holiness and righteousness before him all our days.

LUKE 1: 74-75

Therefore, since we have these promises, dear friends, let us purify ourselves from everything that contaminates body and spirit, perfecting holiness out of reverence for God.

2 CORINTHIANS 7:1

But just as he who called you is holy, so be holy in all you do; for it is written: "Be holy, because I am holy."

1 PETER 1:15-16

JUDGEMENT

For many, the idea of judgement feels scary and damning. But judgement need not scare believers because judgement is when God rewards holiness and punishes evil. Judgement is when God rights wrong and brings justice where injustice has reigned. Like the teacher who gives his students an open-book test because he wants them to learn and do well, God gives us the Bible, his instructions for holy living, because he wants us to learn, do well, and ultimately be well. These instructions are there for us to study and adhere to daily as life tests us. Judgement is simply God rewarding us according to what we learned, what we did, and who we became. That's ultimately a good thing.

God of Justice,

I'm grateful that you reward those who've lived according to your Word. Daily, would you help me to live according to your guidelines so that I can receive the promised reward? Would you help me mature, so I welcome judgement instead of fearing it?

Amen

But I tell you that everyone will have to give account on the day of judgment for every empty word they have spoken. For by your words you will be acquitted, and by your words you will be condemned.

MATTHEW 12:36–37

So, then each of us shall give account of himself to God. Let us not therefore judge one another anymore...

ROMANS 14:12

My conscience is clear, but that does not make me innocent. It is the Lord who judges me.

1 CORINTHIANS 4:4

For we must all appear before the judgment seat of Christ, so that each of us may receive what is due us for the things done while in the body, whether good or bad.

2 CORINTHIANS 5:10

ETERNAL LIFE

As we go about daily life and check things off our 'to do lists,' it's easy to stay focused mostly on the present. Eternal life, in comparison, can feel distant like a faraway, mystical world described in a cherished book. In reality, eternal life is an extension of our present life. Eternal life gifts us a forever home with God (John 14:1–4). This life frees us from death and its destruction. So, each day, as you're caring for your family and checking things off your list, be sure to give God time and space to make a home with you now—in preparation for the eternal life that's to follow.

Everlasting God,

The gift of eternal life is another way you show your love to us. As I work tirelessly to take care of my family's needs, help me to never lose sight of how precious eternal life is. Each day, usher my family into the eternal life and home you've prepared for us.

Amen

The last enemy that shall be destroyed is death.

1 CORINTHIANS 15:26

Give thanks to the Lord, for he is good; his love endures forever.

1 CHRONICLES 16:34

Very truly I tell you, whoever hears my word and believes him who sent me has eternal life and will not be judged but has crossed over from death to life.

JOHN 5:24

The life of mortals is like grass, they flourish like a flower of the field; the wind blows over it and it is gone, and its place remembers it no more. But from everlasting to everlasting the Lord's love is with those who fear him, and his righteousness with their children's children—with those who keep his covenant and remember to obey his precepts.

PSALMS 103:15–18

And this is the testimony: God has given us eternal life, and this life is in his Son.

1 JOHN 5:11

GRACE

Grace is mercy covered with honey. Grace is the unearned favor and blessing from God for all who believe. God covers believers with grace because he understands that we are human beings that consistently mess up. Sometimes it's because we're selfish and sometimes it's because we've been careless. Regardless, God's grace always covers us. In these moments, God gives us a hug instead of a lecture. This grace is a model for how we can mother: lovingly covering our children's messes and knowing when it's best to give them hugs in lieu of lectures. Grace is the gift every child needs to receive from a parent. This gift shows them that they are embraced just as they are. Like honey, grace is always welcomed and always sweet.

Gracious God,

Thank you for all the times you've chosen to cover me with sweet grace. Please help me to cover my children with this same grace, especially when they've purposefully defied me. Please teach me how to be more patient and compassionate.

Amen

But he said to me, "My grace is sufficient for you, for my power is made perfect in weakness." Therefore, I will boast all the more gladly of my weaknesses, so that the power of Christ may rest upon me.

2 CORINTHIANS 12:9

And God is able to make all grace abound to you, so that having all sufficiency in all things at all times, you may abound in every good work.

2 CORINTHIANS 9:8

Let us then approach God's throne of grace with confidence, so that we may receive mercy and find grace to help us in our time of need.

HEBREWS 4:16

The Lord bless you and keep you; the Lord make his face shine on you and be gracious to you; the Lord turn his face toward you and give you peace.

NUMBERS 6:24-26

MARRIAGE

The covenant of marriage is supposed to last a lifetime. In Scripture, God invites us all—women and men—into an everlasting marriage covenant with him. God also invites us into marriage with a spouse, someone who's supposed to love, protect, and cherish us, just like God. Sometimes, these marriages collapse due to selfishness, disagreements, infidelity, addiction, and the like. Maybe you or a loved one has experienced this. Maybe your marriage is good, but in need of some TLC. Or maybe you're a widow or have never been married. Through the highs and lows of our romantic relationships, God assures us that his commitment to us is forever. He is not going anywhere.

Loving God,

Thank you for being the model of what a loving husband looks like. Thank you for loving, protecting, and cherishing me. Help me to know that I don't need to hide any parts of myself from you because your commitment to me is eternal.

Amen

Two are better than one, because they have a good return for their labor: if either of them falls down, one can help the other up. But pity anyone who falls and has no one to help them up.

ECCLESIASTES 4:9–10

Carry each other's burdens, and in this way you will fulfill the law of Christ.

GALATIANS 6:2

Above all, love each other deeply, because love covers over a multitude of sins.

1 PETER 4:8

For your husband is your Maker, whose name is the Lord of hosts; And your Redeemer is the Holy One of Israel, who is called the God of all the earth.

ISAIAH 54:5

SETTING AN EXAMPLE

They may not say it or even realize it, but your children need you to set a positive example of how to live a holistic godly life. They need to see you giving your time and money to those in need. They need to see you putting your phone down, eating healthy food, and caring for your body through exercise. Your children need to see you praying and reading your Bible regularly—outside of church—just as much as they need to see you living out the word. When you lose your temper when interacting with your children, apologize and ask for forgiveness. When they sin against you, express you're hurt and then forgive them. If you want your children to lead holistic, God-honoring lives, then you must set an example.

Dear God,

Thank you for sending Jesus, the ultimate example. His life demonstrated the importance of prayer, solitude, rest, giving, and fellowship. Likewise, help me to be that kind of an example for my family.

Amen

And let us consider how we may spur one another on toward love and good deeds.

HEBREWS 10:24

Even small children are known by their actions, so is their conduct really pure and upright?

PROVERBS 20:11

In everything set them an example by doing what is good. In your teaching show integrity, seriousness.

TITUS 2:7

I have set you an example that you should do as I have done for you.

JOHN 13:15

In the same way, let your light shine before others, that they may see your good deeds and glorify your Father in heaven.

MATTHEW 5:16

To this you were called, because Christ suffered for you, leaving you an example, that you should follow in his steps.

1 PETER 2:21

FORGIVENESS

Extending forgiveness can be hard sometimes—not because you want to hold an offense against someone—but simply because you're hurt. You want to forgive, but your heart aches. In these moments, you must ask God to heal the pain. You must ask God to keep your heart from becoming cold and hard toward the person who hurt you. You must ask God to help your heart to forgive, or maybe—to even want to forgive. An open, forgiving heat enables you to receive and give love to God and others. If you choose to walk in forgiveness, you walk in the fullness of God's forgiveness and love for you. If you choose to walk in unforgiveness, you walk in disobedience and choose separation from God. Which path do you want to walk in?

Forgiving Father,

I want to forgive, but sometimes it's hard. Please heal any hurt, anger, or bitterness in my heart. Help me to see how much you forgive me and help me to choose to walk in forgiveness every day.

Amen

Bear with each other and forgive one another if any of you has a grievance against someone. Forgive as the Lord forgave you.

COLOSSIANS 3:13

Repent, then, and turn to God, so that your sins may be wiped out, that times of refreshing may come from the Lord.

ACTS 3:19

Do not judge, and you will not be judged. Do not condemn, and you will not be condemned. Forgive, and you will be forgiven.

LUKE 6:37

Then Peter came up and said to him, "Lord, how often will my brother sin against me, and I forgive him? As many as seven times?" Jesus said to him, "I do not say to you seven times, but seventy-seven times."

MATTHEW 18:21-22

And when you stand praying, if you hold anything against anyone, forgive them, so that your Father in heaven may forgive you your sins.

MARK 11:25

REPENTANCE

Simply put, repentance is turning away from sin and towards God. Repentance happens when your actions, attitudes, and beliefs change. Humans are drawn to fire's warmth, beauty, and power. Imagine sin as a destructive forest fire you accidentally started. Repentance means that you make every effort never to start a forest fire again. Maybe you vow to never start a campfire near the woods again. Maybe you read books about fire safety and handling fire outdoors and always have the appropriate safety protections on-hand, just in case. In other words, when you understand how destructive sin is, you vow to avoid it and read scriptures so you can learn how dangerous sin is and how best to avoid it. Repentance means your actions, attitude, and beliefs towards sin shift.

Gracious God,

You're so patient with me when I sin. Help me to be patient with myself as my attitude and my actions towards sin shift. I need you to show me how dangerous sin is and give me strategies to avoid it.

Amen

Repent, then, and turn to God, so that your sins may be wiped out, that times of refreshing may come from the Lord.

ACTS 3:19

Whoever conceals their sins does not prosper, but the one who confesses and renounces them finds mercy.

PROVERBS 28:13

Peter replied, "Repent and be baptized, every one of you, in the name of Jesus Christ for the forgiveness of your sins. And you will receive the gift of the Holy Spirit."

ACTS 2:38

In the same way, I tell you, there is rejoicing in the presence of the angels of God over one sinner who repents.

LUKE 15:10

The Lord is not slow in keeping his promise, as some understand slowness. Instead, he is patient with you, not wanting anyone to perish, but everyone to come to repentance.

2 PETER 3:9

SERVICE

We live in a society that prizes personal success over service to others. The idolization of individual success over communal success means that service is either overlooked completely or seen only as an afterthought. Scripture teaches that service is an opportunity to shine the light of God into the spaces and places that most need it. Service can include your family making meals for a family in need, volunteering at a local Boys & Girls Club, or starting a GoFundMe for someone at your job or church with overwhelming medical bills. Sometimes service happens naturally; other times it requires sacrificial time and effort. Either way, serving others is how we demonstrate that we too are God's children. Like Jesus, we are the servants of all.

Giving God,

I'm grateful that Jesus intentionally demonstrated what a life of service looks like. Help me to show my children the beauty of serving others, both when it's convenient and when it's not.

Amen

Do nothing out of selfish ambition or vain conceit. Rather, in humility value others above yourselves, not looking to your own interests but each of you to the interests of the others. In your relationships with one another, have the same mindset as Christ Jesus.

PHILIPPIANS 2:3-5

Each of you should use whatever gift you have received to serve others, as faithful stewards of God's grace in its various forms.

1 PETER 4:10

"For even the Son of Man came not to be served but to serve, and to give His life as a ransom for many."

MARK 10:45

Each of you should use whatever gift you have received to serve others, as faithful stewards of God's grace in its various forms.

PETER 4:10

For we are co-workers in God's service; you are God's field, God's building.

1 CORINTHIANS 3:9

FAITH

Faith is the cornerstone of Christianity and the foundation of a rich life with God. Our faith touches every part of our lives: how we think and how we act. Do we have faith that God is good, no matter what? Do we believe that God is all-powerful, even when circumstances seem to suggest otherwise? Scripture even says it's impossible to please God without faith (Hebrews 11:6). So how do we receive the gift of faith (Ephesians 2:8–9)? By acknowledging its absence and asking God for it. Like the fearful father in Mark 9:24, we can acknowledge that our faith sometimes fades in and out. Like this man, we can pray a simple prayer: "I do believe; help me overcome my unbelief!" As we ask for faith, God promises to gift it to us.

Lord God,

Sometimes I have faith, and sometimes I lack it altogether. Grant me the gift of faith each day. Help me to trust in your goodness and your power—no matter what.

Amen

If you remain in me and my words remain in you, ask whatever you wish, and it will be done for you.

JOHN 15:7

Then Jesus told him, "Because you have seen me, you have believed; blessed are those who have not seen and yet have believed."

JOHN 20:29

If you falter in a time of trouble, how small is your strength!

PROVERBS 24:10

But now, this is what the Lord says— he who created you, Jacob, he who formed you, Israel: "Do not fear, for I have redeemed you; I have summoned you by name; you are mine. When you pass through the waters, I will be with you; and when you pass through the rivers, they will not sweep over you. When you walk through the fire, you will not be burned; the flames will not set you ablaze."

ISAIAH 43:1–2

GUIDANCE

Throughout the Bible, God promises guidance to everyone who asks. Even better, God promises to bless your paths if you ask him for direction. Asking for guidance requires humility because you're admitting that you need help and don't have it all together. God loves when you ask for things with humility because it's his opportunity to show you that his thoughts are higher than your thoughts, and that his ways are higher than your ways (Isaiah 55:8–9). So each day, be sure to ask God for guidance for how to mother your children. Ask God to show you how to help them navigate school and friendships and their budding identities. Remember: God knows what they need more than you do and is eager to provide guidance to you and them.

God,

Thank you for the promise to guide me in every area. I'm especially grateful that you want to guide me as I raise my children. Teach me new ways of thinking and acting that honor how you created my children.

Amen

Show me your ways, Lord, teach me your paths. Guide me in your truth and teach me, or you are God my Savior, and my hope is in you all day long.

PSALMS 25:4–5

Let the morning bring me word of your unfailing love, for I have put my trust in you. Show me the way I should go, for to you I entrust my life.

PSALMS 143:8

How much better to get wisdom than gold, to get insight rather than silver!

PROVERBS 16:16

If you are pleased with me, teach me your ways so I may know you and continue to find favor with you. Remember that this nation is your people.

EXODUS 33:13

In their hearts humans plan their course, but the Lord establishes their steps.

PROVERBS 16:9

THE HOLY SPIRIT

The Holy Spirit is many things to the believer: a teacher, guide, advocate, and more. The Holy Spirit's job is to help believers craft lives that are holy, which means "set apart for God." Think of the Holy Spirit as a life-long tutor who's with you 24/7. If you're having conflict with a friend, you can ask your tutor for wisdom about how to facilitate peace. If you're facing financial struggles, you can ask your lifelong tutor for practical instructions about how to proceed with faith. If you or a family member is facing illness, you can ask your tutor the best path towards wellness: How are you to pray? What is the best eating and exercise routine? As you submit to life-long tutelage under the Holy Spirit, your life won't be perfect, but it will be holy.

Lord God,

I'm grateful that you sent the Holy Spirit to teach me how to live a holy life. Help me to submit to his tutelage every day, in every part of my life.

Amen

Therefore, go and make disciples of all nations, baptizing them in the name of the Father and of the Son and of the Holy Spirit, and teaching them to obey everything I have commanded you. And surely I am with you always, to the very end of the age.

MATTHEW 28:19–20

May the God of hope fill you with all joy and peace in believing, so that you may overflow with hope by the power of the Holy Spirit.

ROMANS 15:13

Do you not know that your bodies are temples of the Holy Spirit, who is in you, whom you have received from God? You are not your own.

1 CORINTHIANS 6:19

But when he, the Spirit of truth, comes, he will guide you into all the truth. He will not speak on his own; he will speak only what he hears, and he will tell you what is yet to come.

JOHN 16:13

And hope does not put us to shame, because God's love has been poured out into our hearts through the Holy Spirit, who has been given to us.

ROMANS 5:5

COURAGE

The Bible recounts stories of women and men who choose courage in the face of persecution, intimidation, and many hardships. In fact, the call to "be strong and courageous" echoes through the pages of Scripture. Rahab chose courage when she lied to the king so she could stand on the side of Jehovah. Mary chose courage when she said yes to mothering Jesus, even though she would become a social pariah. Do you need courage to obey God? Do you need courage to stand up to a boss or politician who is not on God's side? Maybe you need courage to parent in a way your friends and family disagree with. God wants to give you strength and courage.

God,

It's easy to cling to comfort and security instead of courage and the risk it requires. Give me the strength and courage to stand on your side, no matter the cost.

Amen

Rise up; this matter is in your hands. We will support you, so take courage and do it.

EZRA 10:4

Be strong and very courageous. Be careful to obey all the law my servant Moses gave you; do not turn from it to the right or to the left, that you may be successful wherever you go.

JOSHUA 1:7

Lord Almighty, God of Israel, you have revealed this to your servant, saying, "I will build a house for you." So, your servant has found courage to pray this prayer to you.

2 SAMUEL 7:27

But Jesus immediately said to them: "Take courage! It is I. Don't be afraid."

MATTHEW 14:27

The Lord is my shepherd; I shall not want. He makes me lie down in green pastures. He leads me beside still waters. He restores my soul. He leads me in paths of righteousness for his name's sake. Even though I walk through the valley of the shadow of death, I will fear no evil, for you are with me; your rod and your staff, they comfort me.

PSALMS 23:1-4

BLESSINGS

Blessings are God's generosity poured out to us, his children. Blessings are our inheritance. Sometimes we receive them because we've followed God's instructions. Other times, God blesses us, just because. Blessings reveal God's character: God as a doting parent who only wants to bless his children. But he knows that he must withhold some blessings until his children grow up. They must learn to follow their parent's instructions because lifelong wisdom lives there. They must also mature intellectually, spiritually, emotionally, and physically to become ready to receive their inheritance. Once they've matured and learned to follow their parent's instructions, God will not withhold any blessing. Rather, he'll give even more.

Giving God,

Thank you for the blessings you've already given to my family. Teach us to follow your instructions and mature us so we can receive every blessing you have for us.

Amen

Every good and perfect gift is from above, coming down from the Father of the heavenly lights, who does not change like shifting shadows.

JAMES 1:17

Praise be to the God and Father of our Lord Jesus Christ, who has blessed us in the heavenly realms with every spiritual blessing in Christ.

EPHESIANS 1:3

And my God will meet all your needs according to the riches of his glory in Christ Jesus.

PHILIPPIANS 4:19

But blessed is the one who trusts in the Lord, whose confidence is in him. They will be like a tree planted by the water that sends out its roots by the stream. It does not fear when heat comes; its leaves are always green. It has no worries in a year of drought and never fails to bear fruit.

JEREMIAH 17:7–8

You will eat the fruit of your labor; blessings and prosperity will be yours.

PSALMS 128:2

PRAISE

Scripture commands us to praise God, not because God needs our praise, but because we need to praise. Praise is simply applauding God for who he is and what he's done. Praise can look many ways, including giving God thanks, singing songs of thanksgiving, and dancing. Praise is a simple yet powerful act, particularly when you're facing challenging circumstances. Scripture implores us to praise because it focuses our attention on God. Worried? Praise by reciting Psalm 23 or another psalm. Sick? Thank God for loving you and being a miracle-worker. Lonely? Sing songs of praise until your mood shifts and you feel God's presence. In every challenging circumstance, always praise.

Lord God,

I want to learn how to praise you more, especially when I face challenging circumstances. When I'm tempted to live in anxiety and worry, teach me how to recite and sing songs of praise so I can focus on you.

Amen

I lift up my eyes to the hills. From where does my help come? My help comes from the Lord, who made heaven and earth.

PSALMS 121:1–2

Give praise to the Lord, proclaim his name; make known among the nations what he has done.

PSALMS 105:1

Lord, you are my God; I will exalt you and praise your name, for in perfect faithfulness you have done wonderful things, things planned long ago.

ISAIAH 25:1

I waited patiently for the Lord; he turned to me and heard my cry. He lifted me out of the slimy pit, out of the mud and mire; he set my feet on a rock and gave me a firm place to stand. He put a new song in my mouth, a hymn of praise to our God.

Many will see and fear the Lord and put their trust in him.

PSALMS 40:1–3

I will extol the Lord at all times; his praise will always be on my lips. I will glory in the Lord; let the afflicted hear and rejoice.

PSALMS 34:1–2

HUMILITY

As parents, sometimes we reward our children's good behavior. But we don't want our children to behave well just for the reward or simply to avoid punishment. We want them to develop the character that compels them to behave well, despite potential rewards and consequences. This is true when we discuss humility. God wants us to exhibit humility before him and other people, neither to receive a reward nor to avoid a consequence, but simply out of love. Humility is kind of a paradox: if we choose to be humble, we will be exalted, but if we exalt ourselves, we will be humbled. God asks us to be humble because when we exalt ourselves, we step on people and dishonor God. By contrast, when we humble ourselves, we uplift people and honor God. When our character is marked by humility, God gladly exalts and honors us.

Father God,

Help me to be humble before my children, family, friends, and strangers. Teach me to desire humility simply because it honors you.

Amen

Pride goes before destruction, and a haughty spirit before a fall. It is better to be of a lowly spirit with the poor than to divide the spoil with the proud.

PROVERBS 16:18–19

In the same way, you who are younger, submit yourselves to your elders. All of you, clothe yourselves with humility toward one another, because God opposes the proud but shows favor to the humble.

1 PETER 5:5

Now that I, your Lord and Teacher, have washed your feet, you also should wash one another's feet.

JOHN 13:14

Pride brings a person low, but the lowly in spirit gain honor.

PROVERBS 29:23

KINDNESS

It's usually easy to show kindness to friends, family, and colleagues. One of the truest indicators of kindness, though, is how you treat strangers and how you respond to others in less than ideal circumstances. Maybe you're running late to work when someone asks you to buy them food. Do you pause to buy them breakfast or give them money for food? Maybe you're on a much-needed beach vacation when a friend calls, in crisis, asking for help. Do you interrupt your trip to assist? Kindness requires that you give of yourself. That you give time, energy, money, and love to those who need it. Will you choose to extend kindness today and every day?

God,

Thank you for being the blueprint for kindness. Give me the love that undergirds true kindness. Teach me how to display kindness to strangers and loved ones, even when it's inconvenient.

Amen

Those who are kind benefit themselves,
but the cruel bring ruin on themselves.

PROVERBS 11:17

Be devoted to one another in love. Honor one another above yourselves.

ROMANS 12 :10

A kindhearted woman gains honor, but ruthless men gain only wealth.

PROVERBS 11:16

Put on then, as God's chosen ones, holy and beloved, compassionate hearts, kindness, humility, meekness, and patience.

COLOSSIANS 3:12

STRENGTH

We spend most of our lives learning to gain physical, emotional, mental, and spiritual strength. You may work out or see either a therapist or a psychologist. You may attend church or even a small group Bible study. These practices are great—essential, even. But sometimes, your human strength just isn't enough. Sometimes you need to fix a relationship or situation that seems beyond repair. What do you do when you need to rebuild but you have neither the physical, emotional, mental, nor spiritual strength? You pray for supernatural strength. You ask God to overshadow your limited human strength with divine strength. As you pray, you will feel your hope and strength rising.

God,

In Isaiah 40:31, you promise to strengthen those who hope in you. When my human strength is gone, help me to ask for your divine strength and wait until I receive it.

Amen

Finally, be strong in the Lord and in his mighty power.

EPHESIANS 6:10

She is clothed with strength and dignity; she can laugh at the days to come.

PROVERBS 31:25

But the Lord has become my fortress, and my God the rock in whom I take refuge.

PSALMS 94:22

But you, O Lord, are a shield about me, my glory, and the lifter of my head.

PSALMS 3:3

God is within her; she will not fall; God will help her at the break of day.

PSALMS 46:5

GRIEF

Nothing is more gutting than the grief you feel after a loved one passes. It's as if your heart has been squeezed so brutally that only a faint beat remains. This type of grief can leave you wondering if you can go on. In these moments, even prayer can feel intolerable because when you stop to pray, all you feel is pain. Still, in these moments God is close to you and promises to comfort you. All you have to do is sit with God. In these moments, you're free to fully express yourself: to cry, yell, and ask why. You can be real and raw with God as you grieve because God wants to hold you and your grief.

God of Comfort,

Teach me to always sit with you when I grieve. Teach me how to handle grief's ebbs and flows. Show me how to move forward with a heart that no longer feels whole.

Amen

The Lord is close to the brokenhearted and saves those who are crushed in spirit.

PSALMS 34:18

So will it be with the resurrection of the dead. The body that is sown is perishable; it is raised imperishable; it is sown in dishonor; it is raised in glory; it is sown in weakness; it is raised in power; it is sown a natural body; it is raised a spiritual body. If there is a natural body, there is also a spiritual body.

1 CORINTHIANS 15:42–44

He will wipe away every tear from their eyes, and death shall be no more, neither shall there be mourning, nor crying, nor pain anymore, for the former things have passed away.

REVELATION 21:4

The salvation of the righteous is from the Lord; he is their stronghold in the time of trouble.

PSALMS 37:39

TEACHING

Sometimes your child might misbehave in public or get in trouble at school, and you may feel slightly embarrassed. In these moments, you might question your parenting style and wonder if you're a good teacher. Although you can't control your children's behavior, you can control what you teach them, in word and in action. You can teach them the importance of character and model it. You can apologize when you've broken a promise or disciplined them in anger. You can teach them to memorize verses from Proverbs that emphasize honesty and integrity. The more your life aligns with the teachings of Scripture, the more likely they are to become adults who make you proud—in public and in private.

Father God,

Thank you for being a patient teacher. Help me to follow your teachings daily so I can teach my children to do the same. We want to make you proud of us—in public and in private.

Amen

These commandments that I give you today are to be on your hearts. Impress them on your children. Talk about them when you sit at home and when you walk along the road, when you lie down and when you get up.

DEUTERONOMY 6:6–7

And all your children shall be taught by the Lord, and great shall be the peace of your children.

ISAIAH 54:13

In everything set them an example by doing what is good. In your teaching show integrity, seriousness and soundness of speech that cannot be condemned, so that those who oppose you may be ashamed because they have nothing bad to say about us.

TITUS 2:7-8

Teach me your way, O Lord, that I may walk in your truth; unite my heart to fear your name. I give thanks to you, O Lord my God, with my whole heart, and I will glorify your name forever.

PSALMS 86:11-12

PRUDENCE

Prudence is the ability to control and discipline yourself via reason. Think of prudence and wisdom as fraternal twins: similar but different and often found together. When you have prudence, you make decisions based on reason more than emotion. In fact, if you have prudence, you understand that emotions are fleeting and not fully reliable. Can you think of specific areas where your children need to exercise prudence? As a parent, you're tasked with teaching your children how to grow this virtue. If they do 'x,' then what will happen as a result? If they don't do 'x,' then what will happen? Thankfully they can develop prudence over time, as they age and mature. They just need a patient, prudent teacher.

God,

You are the source of all knowledge, wisdom, and prudence. Please give me prudence where I lack it and the wisdom to teach my children how to develop this much-needed virtue.

Amen

I, wisdom, dwell with prudence, and I find knowledge and discretion.

PROVERBS 8:12

The simple believes everything, but the prudent gives thought to his steps.

PROVERBS 14:15

Even a fool who keeps silent is considered wise; when he closes his lips, he is deemed intelligent.

PROVERBS 17:28

My dear brothers and sisters, take note of this: Everyone should be quick to listen, slow to speak and slow to become angry.

JAMES 1:19

Fools show their annoyance at once, but the prudent overlook an insult.

PROVERBS 12:16

HEALING

Throughout the Bible, there are countless examples of people receiving divine healing from God. Whether it's someone being healed of leprosy (Luke 5:12–16) or someone being healed from a deadly fall (Acts 20:7–12), God is shown as a loving, all-powerful healer. In light of this, Scripture encourages us to pray for healing, be it physical, emotional, or spiritual. What's challenging is when healing—especially physical healing—doesn't come. Is God neither loving nor all-powerful then? Or could that mean that another type of healing could be taking place? Could our souls thrive as our physical bodies wither away? Could our trust in God grow even as our bodies prepare for their eternal rest? Can we wrap our minds and hearts around a reality where our complete healing is found in heaven, in God's healing presence?

God,

It's hard to understand why some people don't experience physical healing and others do. However, I still believe in your healing power. Please clearly show my family how you heal physically, emotionally, and spiritually so that we always believe, no matter what.

Amen

Dear friend, I pray that you may enjoy good health and that all may go well with you, even as your soul is getting along well.

3 JOHN 1:2

Heal the sick in it and say to them, "The kingdom of God has come near to you."

LUKE 10:9

"But I will restore you to health and heal your wounds," declares the Lord. "Because you are called an outcast for whom no one cares."

JEREMIAH 30:17

He said to her, "Daughter, your faith has healed you. Go in peace and be freed from your suffering."

MARK 5:34

Lord my God, I called to you for help, and you healed me.

PSALMS 30:2

CHARITY

Charity is the practice of giving to those in need without an expectation of anything in return. The Bible asks us to give so our neighbors can have what they need, and so our hearts can expand to those around us. The word 'charity' also translates as 'love.' Charity is how we love our neighbors, God, and ourselves. When we extend charity, we extend love to our neighbors (1 John 3:17). When we extend charity, we invite prosperity into our lives (Proverbs 11:25). When we extend charity, we are essentially giving to God and will be rewarded for that gift even though it shouldn't be our motive (Proverbs 19:17). In short, charity is good for all parties. Let's not limit it to annual fundraisers. Let's extend charity all year-round.

Giving God,

Charity is your very essence. Help my family become people who are known for our love. Every day show us ways we can extend charity to our neighbors and each other.

Amen

In everything I did, I showed you that by this kind of hard work we must help the weak, remembering the words the Lord Jesus himself said: "It is more blessed to give than to receive."

ACTS 20:35

Whoever is kind to the poor lends to the Lord, and he will reward them for what they have done.

PROVERBS 19:17

If anyone has material possessions and sees a brother or sister in need but has no pity on them, how can the love of God be in that person?

1 JOHN 3:17

All believers were together and had everything in common. They sold property and possessions to give to anyone in need.

ACTS 2:44-5

Do not forget to show hospitality to strangers, for by so doing some people have shown hospitality to angels without knowing it.

HEBREWS 13:2

ENCOURAGEMENT

The meaning of the word 'encouragement' is embedded in its name. Encouragement is being inspired to have courage and confidence. When you're experiencing fear, anxiety, and overwhelm, encouragement fuels you to keep going with hope and faith. Encouragement is light in a dark tunnel and water on a scorching summer day. We all need it—some days more than others. Encouragement can show up in many forms: through a Bible verse, a hymn or worship song, a handwritten note, a friend's assuring hug, and even a meme on social media. Considering this, how can you actively seek encouragement today? How can you actively give it to your children? To your extended family and friends?

Heavenly Father,

Scripture is filled with examples of you encouraging your children to keep following you, even when life gets hard and feels overwhelming. Help me to be a woman who seeks encouragement when I'm fearful and anxious and encourages others when they are, too.

Amen

For everything that was written in the past was written to teach us, so that through the endurance taught in the scriptures and the encouragement they provide we might have hope.

ROMANS 15:4

Therefore, if you have any encouragement from being united with Christ, if any comfort from his love, if any common sharing in the Spirit, if any tenderness and compassion, then make my joy complete by being like-minded, having the same love, being one in spirit and of one mind.

PHILIPPIANS 2:1–2

Therefore encourage one another and build each other up, just as in fact you are doing.

1 THESSALONIANS 5 :11

The metalworker encourages the goldsmith, and the one who smooths with the hammer spurs on the one who strikes the anvil. One says of the welding, "It is good." The other nails down the idol so it will not topple.

ISAIAH 41:7

WORSHIP

Songs are powerful. Have you ever noticed how your mood can shift after singing a favorite song? Singing worship songs is even more powerful because singing praises to God can lift our spirits as well as our emotions. Singing about God's faithfulness shifts the parts of us that have been shrouded in loneliness. Singing about God's power shifts the places within us that have been overwhelmed by fear. Singing about God's love assures us that we are loved, no matter how we feel. Singing worship songs helps our spirits be able to live out worship in our daily lives. This spiritual discipline is essential for us. Consider having a 30-minute worship session with your family once a week. Sing your favorite worship songs and watch how your spirits lift, not just in the moment, but throughout the week.

Father God,

Thank you for the gift of worship. Help me and my family to be disciplined to sing songs of worship regularly. Show us the benefits of this spiritual discipline.

Amen

Therefore, since we are receiving a kingdom that cannot be shaken, let us be thankful, and so worship God acceptably with reverence and awe.

HEBREWS 12:28

Ascribe to the Lord the glory due his name; bring an offering and come before him.Worship the Lord in the splendor of his holiness.

1 CHRONICLES 16:29

God is spirit, and his worshipers must worship in the Spirit and in truth.

JOHN 4:24

You alone are the Lord. You made the heavens, even the highest heavens, and all their starry host, the earth and all that is on it, the seas and all that is in them. You give life to everything, and the multitudes of heaven worship you.

NEHEMIAH 9:6

FAIRNESS

We've heard it many times: life isn't fair. This lack of fairness and justice is visible all around us: in our schools, cities, country, and even our churches and homes. Maybe there's a lack of fairness due to gender, race, education, or socio-economic status. Experiencing injustice is difficult, as is witnessing it. Whom do we turn to? Who will make things right? From the Old Testament to the New Testament, God emphatically declares that he loves justice. Throughout Scripture, God rights injustices and makes crooked paths straight. So, when we or others are being treated unfairly, we can ask God to execute his justice. He promises to bring it. If not now, then certainly later.

Loving God,

Your concern for people and the world is infinite. Help my family to live lives characterized by justice. Help us to be people who bring justice to the places in our cities and country that need it most.

Amen

Blessed are those who act justly, who always do what is right.

PSALMS 106:3

Honest scales and balances belong to the Lord; all the weights in the bag are of his making.

PROVERBS 16:11

My brothers and sisters, believers in our glorious Lord Jesus Christ must not show favoritism.

JAMES 2:1

When justice is done, it brings joy to the righteous but terror to evildoers.

PROVERBS 21:15

TRIBULATIONS

No one likes tribulations, yet intense trouble and suffering are a part of life. They bang on everyone's doors. The irony is that tribulations aren't all doom and gloom. They are where we receive help from God, where we experience God's love and provision, and where we are refined. Whether we're facing a concerning diagnosis, broken relationship, or financial crisis, Scripture reveals that God meets us in troubling times. In 1 Kings 17, God provides for a mother in financial despair who's on the brink of death. In Luke 8:43–48, Jesus heals a woman who's been sick for most of her life. Through these stories and our own stories, God reminds us to come to him when tribulation bangs on our doors. He can craft something good from something bad.

All-Powerful God,

Our darkest tribulations are not strong enough to stop you from creating something good. Help me to believe that you are more powerful than the worst thing imaginable and help me to call on you when my family faces tribulations.

Amen

When times are good, be happy; but when times are bad, consider this: God has made the one as well as the other. Therefore, no one can discover anything about their future.

ECCLESIASTES 7:14

The Lord is good, a stronghold in the day of trouble; he knows those who take refuge in him.

NAHUM 1:7

God is our refuge and strength, an ever-present help in trouble.

PSALMS 46:1

You will surely forget your trouble, recalling it only as waters gone by.

JOB 11:16

I have told you these things, so that in me you may have peace. In this world you will have trouble. But take heart! I have overcome the world.

JOHN 16:33

KEEPING THE SABBATH

Even God rested. Genesis 2 says that after six days of creating the Earth and humankind, God paused to rest. Keeping the Sabbath is choosing to pause and rest amid life's never-ending demands. This tradition creates space for reflection, meditation, and connection. Keeping the Sabbath requires you to trust God that all your work, household tasks, and other responsibilities will still get handled if you pause. This practice enables you to exchange the hustle and bustle of everyday life for God's rest and refreshing presence. On the Sabbath, your family can disconnect from busyness and social media. You can meditate on Scripture and worship together. You can go for a walk and check out the sunrise or the sunset. Keeping the Sabbath helps your family rest physically and reset spiritually each week.

Lord God,

Thank you for giving us the Sabbath to illustrate the importance of rest. Show my family how we can keep the Sabbath more regularly and honor it more fully.

Amen

Then God blessed the seventh day and made it holy, because on it he rested from all the work of creating that he had done.

GENESIS 2:3

If you keep your feet from breaking the Sabbath and from doing as you please on my holy day, if you call the Sabbath a delight and the Lord's holy day honorable, and if you honor it by not going your own way and not doing as you please or speaking idle words, then you will find your joy in the Lord, and I will cause you to ride in triumph on the heights of the land and to feast on the inheritance of your father Jacob.

ISAIAH 58:13-15

There remains, then, a Sabbath-rest for the people of God; or anyone who enters God's rest also rests from their works, just as God did from his.

HEBREWS 4:9-10

Remember the Sabbath day by keeping it holy.

EXODUS 20:8

CALM

We all want a calm, peaceful life. We want to experience harmonious relationships and meaningful work. But life is filled with storms that produce anything but calm. In those moments, we beg God to end our troubles. But often we need to learn to experience calm *within* the storm. We can experience this calm in numerous ways. We can opt for a walk or a run to experience physical calm. We can practice breathing exercises for a few minutes until our bodies still. We can experience the soothing power of Scripture as we read it aloud and meditate on it. We can even sing Scripture. Lastly, we can invite Jesus into the storm and ask him to hold us until it ends. Once we accept that troubling times are inevitable parts of life, we can learn how better to experience calm amid them.

God,

I'm grateful that with you I can experience calm amid any tempest. Teach me how to experience calm and peace, no matter how big the storm.

Amen

Let the peace of Christ rule in your hearts, since as members of one body you were called to peace. And be thankful.

COLOSSIANS 3:15

Peace I leave with you; my peace I give you. I do not give to you as the world gives. Do not let your hearts be troubled and do not be afraid.

JOHN 14:27

But whoever listens to me will live in safety and be at ease, without fear of harm.

PROVERBS 1:33

Therefore, since these facts are undeniable, you ought to calm down and not do anything rash.

ACTS 19:36

FEAR

Fear is a natural human emotion. Whether it's a fear of heights or the fear of being hurt—either physically or emotionally—fear is as natural as the emotional support blankies toddlers cling to. Yet throughout Scripture, God consistently tells us "Do not fear." Fear can prevent us from choosing trust and faith in God. Fear says "You're not safe. You're all alone," while God says "I am with you. I'm taking care of you." Fear says "There's no hope. This is the end," while God says, "Put your trust in me." Fear says "This is scary. I should stop now," while God says "When you pass through the waters, I will be with you; and when you pass through the rivers, they will not sweep over you. (Isaiah 43:2)." Each day holds opportunities to either listen to fear or listen to God. Which will you choose?

Loving God,

When life gets hard and fear talks to me, help me to listen to you. Teach me to trust that you are always with me, actively caring for me.

Amen

Though an army besiege me, my heart will not fear; though war break out against me, even then I will be confident.

PSALMS 27:3

When I am afraid, I put my trust in you.

PSALMS 56:3

For the Spirit God gave us does not make us timid, but gives us power, love, and self-discipline.

2 TIMOTHY 1:7

So do not fear, for I am with you; do not be dismayed, for I am your God. I will strengthen you and help you; I will uphold you with my righteous right hand.

ISAIAH 41:10

You will not fear the terror of night, nor the arrow that flies by day.

PSALMS 91:5

GRATITUDE

It's easy to feel and express gratitude when everything is going well. When your loved ones are healthy, your wants and needs are met, and you feel fulfilled, gratitude comes easily. However, expressing gratitude when things are difficult is as challenging as it is necessary. Gratitude is the life raft you need—not just to keep going—but to keep going with hope. Making a list of 20–30 things you're grateful for will remind you of your blessings. This list will shift your focus from all the bad to all the good. Expressing gratitude helps you focus on facts, not feelings. One fact is that you are seen and loved by God and others. Another fact is that the more you express gratitude, the more you will feel it.

Father God,

Sometimes I doubt and overlook your care for me. Sometimes I don't express my gratitude. Give me eyes to see how much you and others love me. Help me to express my gratitude daily.

Amen

For from him and through him and to him are all things. To him be glory forever. Amen.

ROMANS 11:36

Bless the Lord, O my soul, and forget not all his benefits.

PSALMS 103:2

I will give thanks to the Lord because of his righteousness; I will sing the praises of the name of the Lord Most High.

PSALMS 7:17

At midnight I rise to give you thanks for your righteous laws.

PSALMS 119:62

Sing to the Lord with grateful praise; make music to our God on the harp.

PSALMS 100:1

MIRACLES

Miracles happen. Miracles don't *always* happen, though. That's why it's hard for some of us to pray for them. What if we pray for a miracle and it never arrives? Will the disappointment keep us from praying again? Or will we dare to pray again? Can we believe that sometimes God doesn't give us a miracle now so we can receive a bigger miracle later? Whether you've ever experienced one or not, it's important to never stop asking. When you ask, though, have faith that God is all-powerful and that God's goodness isn't limited to a specific outcome. The truth is that we can't control whether we experience miracles or not. But we can control if we ask for them.

Powerful God,

Nothing is too hard for you. Help me to always ask for miracles, and help me to ask in faith, trusting that you love me and want only to give me good things.

Amen

He performs wonders that cannot be fathomed, miracles that cannot be counted.

JOB 5:9

I will remember the deeds of the Lord; yes, I will remember your miracles of long ago.

PSALMS 77:11

So again, I ask, does God give you his Spirit and work miracles among you by the works of the law, or by your believing what you heard?

GALATIANS 3:5

The disciples were even more amazed, and said to each other, "Who then can be saved?" Jesus looked at them and said, "With man this is impossible, but not with God; all things are possible with God."

MARK 10:26–27

He is the one you praise; he is your God, who performed for you those great and awesome wonders you saw with your own eyes.

DEUTERONOMY 10:21

FAMILY

There's nothing like family. Our families establish the foundations in our lives and when healthy—support us throughout our entire lives. As believers we have two sets of family: our biological family and our spiritual family, the family of God. (Thankfully, sometimes these are the same.) Both families are supposed to emulate God's love to us, and both are supposed to refine our character. As a mother, you can give your children a sense of safety and security through their biological family and their spiritual family. You can take them to K–12 school and to Sunday school. You can watch them develop supportive life-long relationships with their first cousins and the kids in their church youth group. When you and your children regularly connect with your biological and spiritual families, your family will be richer and sweeter as a result.

Father God,

Thank you for the gift of biological and spiritual families. Help my biological family to stay closely connected with the extended family of God you've given us.

Amen

If anyone does not know how to manage his own family, how can he take care of God's church?

1 TIMOTHY 3:5

How good and pleasant it is when God's people live together in unity!

PSALMS 133:1

Anyone who does not provide for their relatives, and especially for their own household, has denied the faith and is worse than an unbeliever.

1 TIMOTHY 5:8

Therefore, as we have opportunity, let us do good to all people, especially to those who belong to the family of believers.

GALATIANS 6:10

All your children will be taught by the Lord, and great will be their peace.

ISAIAH 54:13

FINAL PRAYER

Heavenly Father,

I'm grateful that your primary purpose for me is to experience love. Help me to love and experience loving relationships as I love my children and do my purpose-work outside of my home.

Amen

I can do all this through him who gives me strength.

PHILIPPIANS 4:13